It's Time yoU Fucking Flew!

For D, K and G, the best three!

All rights are reserved.
No part of this publication may be reproduced, stored in a retrieval system or transmitted in any form or by any means, electronic, mechanical, photocopying, recording or otherwise, without prior permission of Three Leaps Media.

Typography: Zubilo Black, Iowan Old Style
Text & illustrations Copyright ©2016
by Doc Rooster Hardnip, the Third.
All rights reserved.
Published by Three Leaps Media.
www.threeleaps.com

ISBN 978-0-9977261-0-7
First Edition

E-book ISBN 978-0-9977261-1-4

4 YOU!

The years flown.
Why not you?

Get a clue
It's time you fucking flew!
Baby ewe, get your shoes.

Cut the slack.
Do you need a nut slap?

No coddle!
Don't dawdle!
Vacate, Cupcake!
Grow a pair. No highchair.

Feet on floor.
Out the door.
You're not 2.
You're 24!

Grow up, baby lamb, SCRAM!
Think you can fly
    jammed in a pram,
 swaddled safe in tissues?

Tender ears, now listen:
    No one, none, gives a damn,
      about your wee issues.

Warning! Trigger Alert:
Words will ruffle your skirt.
Your mangina might hurt.

Ouch? Get the fuck
    outta the pouch.

Stop sucking at the teat,
stand on your own two feet.

Suck it up, buttercup.

You used to run away
   on bad, very bad days.

Now you just stew and simmer,
    in a dither,
   sunk, down deep
      in a funk.

You are not a snowflake,
  nor a fucking mistake.
Be agile, not fragile.
  Don't pout! Climb the fuck out!

Find a role for your
  heart, mind, and soul.
  Time for you to deploy, little boy.

Oh, the places you won't know,
  unless you,
    man-the-fuck-up,
    and roll!

You can't fly, with each eye
making love to your screen,
each wing,
wrapping your peen.
You have come,
yet not sprung,
not went
from the basement.

ULTRA HIGH D 4k ALL DAY

Always on, never gone
forlorn, buried in porn,
eve 'til morn,
streaming every minute,
wanking without limit.

Solo, oh so lonely.
You will woo her never...
to the sewer tethered.

Be a man worthy borne –
Unplug the fucking porn!

Wonder why
you don't fly?
Hear the news:
"Not Benign!"

Right here, your MRI,
shows vertebrae 24 and nine,
but, not one. fucking. spine.
"No backbone, lacking stones."

Oh wait, look deep, you wuss.
They're there!
Bent, buried, smushed,
...by your giant, fucking uterus!

Your spinal atrophy, and mangi-
na-itis, needs massive surgery,
double-douche-otomy.

For a spine so crooked,
no pill will erect it.
Only one therapy-
"Man the fuck up,"
daily.

It's time you
fucking flew,
yet three emus
weigh less
than you do.

Your BMI
too heavy to fly?
Too much booze,
everyday.
Your best friends:
Jim, Jack, José.

You know how to get high,
but will you ever fly?

Get up, off your fat hind,
leave your bullshit behind.

With wings too weak to fly.
and muscle tone so low,
Do you even lift, bro?

Hit the gym. Run, row, swim.
Pull, press, lunge, bench, squat sit,
hard core or try 'CrossFit'.

Pick and roll, pivot, pass-
Get off your lazy ass.
You only need one plan:
Lift as much as you can.

But you will...
gain no testosterone
while chatting on the phone.

And...
those who hijack squat racks
to hurl 5 pound curls,
impress no girls.

Should you splay on a bench
texting bae? No effing way!
It's never, e'er thumb day!

And...never ever,
no way ev'r,
fucking,
skip leg day!

When you give it your all
with racket, weight or ball,
you'll be drenched, dripping wet.
To the showers! No sweat.

Peter Piper didn't get to pick
his pecker, thin or thick.
Neither do you! Why stew?

No worries, none at all!
Short, stubby, ugly, tall,
bald or with a hoodie,
a peen's a peen,
no matter how small
or tall your woody.

No matter how much stick,
just don't be a huge prick!

No more tears.
Get in gear —
no training wheels,
forget your feels.

Take your emo cargo,
Go, get lost,
like Nemo!

Be a man, Peter Pan.
No time for you to stew
and spew that you've
been screwed.

Here's the scoop:
Don't droop!
Get off my fucking stoop!

Time you went, go baby go,
in heat, sleet, or cyclone,

Creep or leap,
Fast or slow,
Time you went,

Lease a high rise, loft space,
chopped up, Italianate,
brown stone-
hiptown or down,
a great, Section 8 rate,
in basement tenement,
art deco or ghetto.

Buy a loft condo? No!
You know you have no dough!

But you still need to go.
Land hard or soft, just get aloft.
Crash anywhere, don't care

...just not here!

Take a bus.
　Take the tube.
　　Ride a rail or choo choo.

　　Don't be lame, take the train
　　　to Maine, Spain, or Ft. Wayne,
　　　　Greece, Nice, Reno or Rome,
　　　　　Just get out of my home.

　　Ride a chartreuse caboose,
　　　elk or moose, fly Spruce Goose.
　　　　No papoose nor excuse,
　　　　　just VAMOOSE!

　　　Or take the tram, just scram!
　　　　It doesn't matter how.
　　　　　Just get the fuck out,

　　　　　　NOW!

Kayak to Kalamazoo, canoe to Timbuktu, or paddle to Peru. Shove off, Adieu! On your way!

No delay. Cast away.

Now,

shoo,
shoo,
shoo!

Hip, Hip, Hooray!!!

Well,
   wait.

On second thought,
          maybe not.

Maybe stay
      one more day,
          li'l bae bae.

You can go...

Tomorrow?

www.ingramcontent.com/pod-product-compliance
Lightning Source LLC
Chambersburg PA
CBHW041226040426
42444CB00002B/64